Identification of Flies Illustrated on Front Cover

Van Luven, Red

Muddler

Bucktail Yellow Caddis

Dark Mossback Nymph

Grey Damsel Nymph

Cahill Flymph

Hare's Ear Flymph, Dark

Blue Charm   Green Damsel Nymph

Tups Flymph

Iron Blue Flymph

Parmachene Belle

Royal Coachman, Wet

Olive May-fly Nymph

Adams, Wet

Little Whitefish

Sports Illustrated
FLY FISHING

The Sports Illustrated Library

BOOKS ON TEAM SPORTS

Baseball   Basketball   Ice Hockey   Football

BOOKS ON INDIVIDUAL SPORTS

Badminton   Golf   Skiing
Fencing   Horseback Riding   Squash
Fly Fishing   The Shotgun   Tennis
Gaited Riding   Shotgun Sports   Track and Field: Running Events

BOOKS ON WATER SPORTS

Better Boating   Junior Sailing   Swimming
Diving   Small Boat Sailing

SPECIAL BOOKS

Dog Training   Safe Driving

Sports Illustrated
FLY FISHING

By VERNON S. HIDY
and the Editors of
Sports Illustrated

Illustrations by
A. Ravielli
and Kyuzo Tsugami

J. B. LIPPINCOTT COMPANY
Philadelphia and New York

U.S. Library of Congress Cataloging in Publication Data

Hidy, Vernon S
    Sports illustrated fly fishing.

    First ed. published in 1961 under title: Book of
wet-fly fishing.
    1. Fly fishing. I. Sports illustrated (Chicago) II. Title.
SH456.H54   1972   799.1'2   74-38908
ISBN-0-397-00859-7
ISBN-0-397-00858-9 (pbk.)

Photographs from *Sports Illustrated*, © Time Inc.

Cover photograph: Walter Kaufman

Photographs on pages 14, 18, 28, 52, 70 and 82:
Vernon S. Hidy

Photographs on pages 78 and 88:
Pete Turner, *Sports Illustrated*

Preface

WELCOME to the delightful sport of fly fishing, a livelier and more delicate approach to catching fish. You will find that each cast brings the possibility of sudden and, at times, violent action. In addition to the pleasures of anticipation and suspense you will enjoy using the more sportsmanlike techniques that offer some advantages to your quarry. The smallness of the hook, the light tippets and various hidden or visible natural obstacles give many fish good chances to escape.

The fellowship of the fly extends around the world and includes the treasures of angling literature. Collecting angling books can be a valuable parallel pastime because such books contain information and knowledge gained by many experienced anglers who have explored a great variety of water and observed the skill of master anglers.

For many men fly fishing is something of a philosophy and a way of life which includes leisurely meadow streams as well as the treacherous, boulder-strewn rapids where the heavy trout often leap and break away. As a fly fisherman you will breathe the blended fragrances of pine, honeysuckle and sweetbriar, and enjoy intimate close-ups of deer, otter, mergansers, snakes and pink columbines, which one angler described as taverns for hummingbirds.

Good luck! . . . on the ledges beside the deeps and on the polished stones of the shallows beside the fast, dark riffles. Oftentimes your trout stream will come alive at sunset with trout, nighthawks and swallows feeding on a beautiful May fly—say the Green Drake or the Pale Evening Dun— floating on currents touched with lavender and gold.

V. S. HIDY

On the Fly Water
Silver Creek, Idaho
September, 1971

Contents

PREFACE   9

1. THE ART OF FLY FISHING   15

2. TROUT STREAM INSECTS   19
May Fly   20
Caddis Fly   21
Stone Fly   22
Midge, Mosquito, Gnat, Crane Fly   23
Damsel Fly, Dragonfly   24
Fish Fly, Alder Fly, Dobson Fly   25
Land-bred Insects   26

3. STRATEGY ON THE STREAM   29
A Pool's Hidden Hazards   35
Tactics for Quiet Water   39
Tricks in Mixed Water   42
Fishing a Big Pool   45

4. LEARNING TO CAST   53
The Grip   55
The Overhead Cast   57
The Side-arm Cast   62
The Roll Cast   66

5. LINES, LEADERS AND KNOTS   71
Lines   71
Leaders   73
Knots   75
Hooks   76

6. NYMPH FISHING   79

7. THE DRY FLY   83
    USING THE WIND   84
    CASTING UPSTREAM   85
        RETRIEVING LINE   85
    CASTING DOWNSTREAM   86
        RETRIEVING LINE   87

8. CHOICE OF FLIES   89
    TYPES OF DRY FLIES   91
    STREAMERS AND BUCKTAILS   92

Sports Illustrated
FLY FISHING

1
The Art of
Fly Fishing

AS described in the following pages, the fly fisherman aspires to deceive fish with imitations of its natural food presented in a manner that simulates the behavior of the nymphs, flymphs, floating flies, drowned flies and darting minnows which fish eat.

A nymph is a larva of an aquatic insect such as the May fly, caddis fly, mosquito and dragonfly. Their wings unfold when the insect leaves the water for the air.

A flymph is any insect in the act of hatching in the water. This dramatic stage of their life cycle brings them swimming up to the surface where they take wing as flies immediately or float momentarily in or on the surface film to dry their wings.

Floating flies imitated by the fly fisherman consist of any aquatic or terrestrial (land-bred) insects indigenous to a

15

particular stream, river or lake. Drowned flies are any of these insects struggling or inert beneath the surface.

Streamers and bucktail flies are used to imitate the minnows and small fry eaten by fish.

A fly fisherman's success depends to a great extent upon his knowledge of the insects most prevalent on the water or in the water at the time he is fishing his artificial flies. Some anglers use "attractor" flies such as the Royal Coachman, or Wickham's Fancy, but the "deceiver" flies such as the Blue Dun, Light Cahill or March Brown are far more effective when the trout are selective, as they often are, in their feeding.

The game of fly fishing is, then, concerned with the size, form, color and behavior of the trout's food in or on the water. The best fly fishermen are, therefore, amateur entomologists and stream strategists who understand the characteristics and behavior of both insects and trout. With some practice and experience you will be able to cast and maneuver the dry fly so it will bounce, skitter, dance or float cleanly without drag. You will also be able to catch trout on the nymph fished deep in the water and the more lively, trout-teasing flymph struggling up through the water in full view of the fish and, oftentimes, the fisherman.

The novice fly fisherman can usually win trout rather easily with streamers and bucktails such as the Gray Ghost, Mickey Finn and Muddler Minnow. Do not be misled, however, by early success in catching the larger, predatory fish on these lures. Streamer fishing is enjoyable, but most fly fishermen consider this of minor importance compared to the other techniques that have greater appeal to both the fish and the fishermen.

The traditional wet fly, unlike the flymph, is tied with a wing which imitates drowned insects of any kind drifting naturally with the current or struggling to regain the surface. Some fishermen tie one pattern of wet fly on the end of the leader and another pattern of wet fly (or dry fly) some 20 or 24 inches above the tail fly. By casting across the stream

16

you can maneuver both flies into pockets and cross-currents as your cast swings downstream, catching individual trout on either fly or doubles when two trout are hooked simultaneously. Many experienced anglers frown upon the use of a dropper fly, but the novice should know about it and explore its possibilities during the early stages of his fishing career.

The Brown Hackle is a deadly general-purpose fly whose body possesses the bronzed effect of beetles and whose hackles will "swim" in the currents like the legs of a struggling insect.

2

Trout Stream Insects

ARTFUL presentation of a fly is easier for the angler who understands the behavior and identity of trout stream insects. The entomology offered here gives only the most significant differences and similarities between insects. Trout eat with their eyes, so to speak, sensing and appreciating naturalness of both the fly and the *behavior* of the fly. Therefore, the angler who can coax a fly to behave naturally must understand the aquatic idiosyncrasies of various insects. He must know what fly to use, how to present it, and *why*.

A lifetime champion of the wet fly, the late G. E. M. Skues, wrote: "The indications which tell your dry-fly angler when to strike are clear and unmistakable, but those which bid a wet-fly man raise his rod point and draw in the steel are frequently so subtle, so evanescent and impalpable to the senses, that when the bending rod assures him that he has divined aright, he feels an ecstasy as though he had performed a miracle each time."

The insects most often eaten by trout come under the following orders:

May fly . . . *Ephemeroptera*
caddis fly . . . *Trichoptera*
stone fly . . . *Plecoptera*
mosquitoes, gnats,
midges, crane fly . . . *Diptera*
ants, bees . . . *Hymenoptera*
grasshoppers . . . *Orthoptera*
dragonfly, damsel fly . . . *Odonata*
fish fly alder fly . . . *Megaloptera*
beetles . . . *Coleoptera*

May fly

MAY FLY

The May fly deserves first mention because its universal appeal to trout has endeared it to all fly fishermen. Jaunty swimmers, the nymphs are all aquatic. Most species swim upward through the water to hatch, tantalizing trout and offering the angler a fine chance to match the struggling flymph with a facsimile in size, form, color and hackle-leg action.

Stage two, the subimago on the surface, calls for a dry fly, as does stage three, the imago or spinner stage of mating and egg-laying. The Gordon Quill, March Brown, Blue Dun, the Cahills and Pink Lady are deservedly famous fly patterns tied with upright wings characteristic of these two stages and designed to float.

Stage four, the spent spinner, brings the wet fly into play for imitating the struggling, drowning insect.

20

Any species of May fly may hatch intermittently over a period of several days. Tuesday's hatching flymph, for example, may be Thursday's spent spinner in the water simultaneously with Thursday's batch of hatching flymphs. Some noted anglers have fished many May fly imitations on the stream theory that a wet fly could represent either the ascending flymph of stage one or the drowning fly of stage four. Such patterns are tied without a wing and a soft or medium hackle, usually a blue dun or honey dun.

caddis fly

CADDIS FLY

So beloved by trout they often eat him case and all, the caddis larva is the gifted architect and engineer any angler may see on the bed of almost any stream or lake. As the larva matures through stage one he enlarges his camouflaged home until he reaches the pupal stage two. Then he seals off the entrance for about two weeks, finally emerging as an exciting swimmer in full view of the trout as described and illustrated in Chapter 3.

This significant similarity to the hatching May fly flymph makes the ascending insect movement simulated by the Leisenring Lift (see page 49) important to a wet-fly angler, for all trout understand it. Also, the fact that the food is *es-*

caddis larva in case

caping somehow triggers otherwise hesitant trout into striking, often just beneath the surface with a deliberate, twisting satisfaction.

The descending fly, also, is a valid wet-fly tactic, for the female of some caddis species crawls or swims down into the water to deposit her eggs after mating. The Hare's Ear, Dark or Light, for instance, is often taken soon after it touches the water since it has a natural counterpart in the female caddis impassioned by instinct to reach an underwater rock, deposit her eggs and perpetuate the species.

Though some anglers moisten a wet fly immediately after knotting it to their leader, it can be sound stream strategy to cast the fly dry and submerge it by giving the leader a pull or two while it is still upstream from the position of a trout. It will possess a delicate, silvery film of air which disappears after a trout takes it or after it becomes well soaked. You may speculate upon the mysterious powers of the fur-bodied flies by comparing them, under water, with any caddis fly you catch and submerge for research purposes. Trout who discover such a fly approaching them will often take it at any depth, so be prepared for action any instant. Also, changing to a fresh fly after catching a fish, is any reasonable wet-fly angler's prerogative.

stone fly

STONE FLY

Three centuries ago Charles Cotton wrote in *The Compleat Angler* of the trout's greed for stone flies. "Matadores for trout and grayling," he called them, "remarkable, both for their size . . . and for the execution they do." Big and durable enough for impaling on a hook, the natural fly is often dapped, floated, or drifted by bait fishermen with impressive results. From the Adirondacks to the Rockies and Cascades, the stone fly has been and will always be a charmer of trout and fly fishermen.

The mated flies crawl about, fly over or simply fall to the water, sometimes in pairs. The eggs are deposited on the water by the flying or floating female and the cycle begins again when the eggs adhere somewhere on the stream bed near where they are dropped, for they are remarkably adhesive.

Quite properly, the stone fly is usually fished as a dry fly. A heavy, thick-bodied fly, it rests low in the water right in the surface film. During the day, however, trout cannot be coaxed to the surface as readily as one might prefer, and at such times a sunken stone fly may produce, for it is one of the choicest morsels on any river for trout of all sizes.

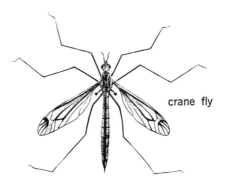

crane fly

MIDGE, MOSQUITO, GNAT, CRANE FLY

An order of insects often ignored by fly fishermen due to the smallness of the larva and pupa, the Diptera are nonetheless essential for deceiving trout under those conditions where the fish are feeding selectively, as they frequently do in the still water of lakes and ponds where the Diptera abound.

In recent years, when nylon tippets as fine as .0039 and .0041 have been available, midge fishing has gained adherents since leader points this small are vital to success when fishing flies as small as 18, 20 and 22, either dry or wet.

The crane fly is a large-scale version of the mosquito. Some are aquatic, some spend just the larval stage in the water and pupate on land. The adult female dips to the water to deposit her eggs.

The deer fly has characteristic mottled wings with legs and body both thicker and shorter than the crane fly.

dragonfly

DAMSEL FLY, DRAGONFLY

Similar in design, with protruding, segmented tube-like bodies and iridescent, transparent wings, these two flies also have similar life cycles. The smaller damsel fly is not as fast a flyer nor as powerful as the dragonfly but both are superb flyers adept at catching and killing lesser insects in mid-air.

fish fly

FISH FLY, ALDER FLY, DOBSON FLY

These trout stream insects resemble each other in that their larvae are all aquatic, similar in appearance but different in shape. The larva of the dobson fly, known as the hellgrammite, is a formidable-looking black creature which grows to a length of 2 or 3 inches. In the summer it crawls ashore and pupates under logs or stones. As adults the dobson flies are nocturnal, noisy flyers, the largest of all trout stream insects.

fish fly larva

The fish fly larva is similar to but smaller than the hellgrammite and it, too, pupates on land.

The alder is a dark-winged fly and long a favorite of the wet-fly fisherman. They are more abundant, as a rule, than the fish fly or the dobson, for both the nymphs and the adult flies constitute an important part of the trout's diet in many streams.

An oddity of the fish fly and the alder fly is that the females lay their eggs on the undersides of protruding logs, rocks and bridges so that the larvae fall to the water when they hatch.

Japanese beetle

LAND-BRED INSECTS

The various insects discussed on this page are all land-bred. Consequently, their only interest to fly fishermen is their availability to trout through the air. The beetles, ants, bees and grasshoppers are particular favorites of the fly fisherman as dry flies, of course, for these insects often float momentarily when they are blown into or fall upon the water. Poor swimmers, they are soon sucked beneath the surface by the currents or the trout. There, if they survive, they kick their legs and struggle for a while in the manner of a drowning stone fly or even a swimming caddis.

wasp

Like the big stone flies, the beetles and grasshoppers are large enough to be tossed into the currents for locating trout, a useful tactic on those days when the angler is anxious for a big one. The type of rise will usually reveal the size of the fish. Once a big trout is located the angler has gained valuable knowledge and may adjust his leader, his fly and his stream strategy to fit the situation.

grasshopper

ant

3
Strategy on the Stream

ALL who fish for trout with an artificial fly will agree that
the really great fascination of the sport lies in the challenging problems of stream strategy. The strategist, in the
ultimate, reckons not only with the habits and moods of
the trout and the behavior of its insect food but also with
the whole character of each stretch of stream: the speed
of the currents, the depth of water, the variations in pools
and riffles, the surface winds, the sunlight and shadow and
an infinity of immobile stage props—trees, brush, rocks and
logs.

The real reward of the observing and skillful angler lies
in his ability to plan an attack that penetrates the natural
defenses of the trout, tempts it to strike his lure and
brings it through obstacles to the net. The angler who
twitches minnow-like bucktails or streamers is counting for
his sport on the capacity of such lures to excite the
rapacity of the trout. The fisherman who uses larval-type,

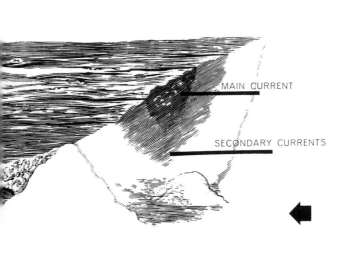

MAIN CURRENT

SECONDARY CURRENTS

weighted nymphs, splashing them into the water so that they plummet to the bottom, is counting for sport on the fundamental hunger of the fish. The dry-fly angler seeks to deceive rising trout at the surface. The angler who aspires to the pleasures of flymph and wet-fly fishing carries out his intrigue against the trout with feathers fragile and exuberant enough to create the illusion of an insect alive *in* the water.

The dry fly's bushy, stiff hackles enable it to ride on the surface film. The wet fly's sparser, softer hackle fibers quiver and kick beneath the surface. As the dry fly can be bounced or twitched about the surface to tantalize trout, so the flymph and wet fly can be maneuvered in the water to act alive. Master angler James E. Leisenring hooked trout at the surface with his Black Ants and beetle-like Brown Hackles, and as his fly descended and moved at various depths, but most often he hooked trout as the fly was rising to the surface. He used the pressure of the currents to activate the hackle fibers so that the fly moved with the *joie de vivre* of the insects themselves. He presented a fly, as he put it, "Naturally, so that the trout will enjoy and appreciate it."

Leisenring took more than a lucky share of trout—and larger trout—because he understood not only the behavior of the fish but also the *behavior* of its food on and *in* the water. He knew where the trout were in various types of water, and he adjusted his techniques to fit the changing character of the water. Equally important, he selected a strategic position on the stream that enabled him to present a fly temptingly to the fish and to play the fish with ease and convenience once it had been hooked. On the following pages you will learn the fine points of stream strategy, tactic by tactic, as they apply to typical stream conditions. First, however, you should know something of the basic ecological features of the water as all experienced anglers understand them.

The currents of a stream, illustrated on page 31 in the

cutaway of a stretch of typical trout water, are food lanes and trout are attracted to them by hunger. Other factors, such as the urge to protect themselves, may divert the trout but, in the main, fish are found where the food is.

Main current as a rule carries the bulk of the food supply during the day, whether insects are hatching or not. Stray insects such as beetles, bees and ants that are blown into or drop to any part of the surface of the stream are usually drawn into the main current.

Secondary currents of lesser velocity at the sides of the main current are the areas generally preferred by trout, since the fish can hold its position in such areas with less effort. Hovering in the secondary current, the trout can swerve into the main current for insects going by or move into quieter water where, if it is deep, the trout may forage for nymphs or struggling insects. During the day trout usually shun the shallows, which offer little concealment from predators.

In fishing uncomplicated water, cast first into the relatively quiet water short of the main current. Such an area is not as likely to hold trout as the lane of secondary velocity farther out, where the broken surface water offers better concealment from two of their main enemies, the osprey and the fisherman, and where the trout can wait for food sweeping by in the main current. But the quiet water sometimes does yield trout; in any case, if the fly is cast there first, then advanced, cast by cast, into more promising areas, the trout, wherever it is, will see the fly before it sees either the leader or the more disturbing ripples and shadows made by the line.

When the angler advances his fly beyond the main current, as on page 31, he runs into a common, recurring problem: drag. Any fast current that drags on line or leader causes the fly to move unnaturally fast. Sometimes the simple expedient of holding the rod high so that the line enters the water beyond the main current solves the problem.

Often, however, when fishing beyond the main current, you must resort to a maneuver known as "mending" your cast. To mend your cast, you first release a little slack line through the guides. Then, by simply flicking your wrist, you impart a circling motion to the tip of your rod, which will throw a loop of the slack line upstream. With this extra slack on the water, your fly for a little time is undisturbed and unaffected by drag.

If you are fishing a rich wilderness area, or any stream recently stocked with small fish, you can at times fish carelessly, unmindful of drag, and still take trout. From such carefree luck you might come to assume, quite logically, that drag is not a deterrent to catching trout. Indeed, almost any size or pattern of fly pulled across the water or beneath it may sometimes attract wilderness trout, since they are often so abundant and food consequently so scarce that they will fight for your fly. Even among the wildest trout, however, you may observe that it is the smaller fish that are most easily deceived.

As fish mature—especially those in our more heavily fished waters—they become increasingly sensitive to drag and other unnatural actions of a fraudulent fly that signal your presence. Whatever the nature of the trout stock, you should always try to minimize drag, use heavy leaders only when necessary, always wade cautiously and avoid disturbances caused by wading, casting unnatural shadows on the water and making sudden movements within view of fish. Though these seem to be inconsequential matters, such violations can spook the more desirable trout. Those two classic challengers, the educated browns and the rainbows, are particularly wary. An oversight of the streamside rules will bring a penalty to the angler as surely as rules violations do to participants in other sports.

If the structure of streams were as simple as the one in the drawing, there would be little more you would need to know than the behavior of trout, their food and the effects of currents. But few streams are this simple, and on the following pages the finer points of strategy are covered as they apply to the true, complicated character of typical streams.

A POOL'S HIDDEN HAZARDS

The stream illustrated on pages 36–37 presents a fairly common but always intriguing problem of strategy. The moment you approach the bank of the pool shown in the foreground, you watch for trout feeding at the surface. If there is no surface activity, you can still presume trout are feeding beneath the surface, as they do most of the time on all streams. On a pool which looks as promising as this one, a well-presented fly could produce a fish almost anywhere. And here, as on many pools of medium size, you might cast from any of several positions. Your choice of position—indeed, your whole plan of attack—depends on what your ambitions are. Will you settle for any fish, or do you want a large one, perhaps the largest in the pool?

If you want a large trout, the place to present your fly is near the half-submerged rock on the far side of the main current. On the downstream side of this rock, decently concealed from predators by the broken water eddying around it, a trout can hover with ease on the edge of the food-laden current. Logic would indicate that the trout by the rock is a good one. The best trout are usually found in the best places.

You can cast to the rock from the bank in the foreground—but should you? If you reconnoiter along the bank, you will notice sunken logs crisscrossed out in the stream. Below these, the current smashes into driftwood piled against the bank and sweeps into the riffle below. A large trout played from the near bank could create crisis after crisis amidst these obstacles and be lost at the logs, the driftwood or in the fast water below.

If you can get to it, the small island just beyond the

rock is a far better casting position. On the island you
would not be casting across the main current. There would
be no drag, and the shorter cast from this spot would enable you to present the fly more temptingly. Moreover,
once you hooked a fish from the island, the pull of your
rod would be *away* from the logs. The island, therefore,
is your choice.

The fast riffle between the bank and the island is deep
and impassable, but farther downstream you have access
across broad shallows. As you wade to the island, you will
note that both the shallows and the deep riffle seem free
of obstacles—a clear path for both the trout and you to the

big water below, where a large fish can be played, exhausted and netted.

Ready now on the island, standing well back, you cast upstream so that your fly sinks before it drifts back to the rock. You guide the fly past the side of the rock away from you, in the current that brings food to the trout. As the fly passes the rock, you raise your rod tip with a slow, gradual motion that causes the fly to rise naturally toward the surface. You pivot your body, following through with the lifting motion, until the fly reaches the surface 6 or 8 feet past the rock. The trout may strike just below the rock or he may follow the fly downstream to inspect it.

Your lifting motion imparts a lifelike movement to the hackle fibers and forces a decision from the trout, since the fly is escaping in a way that the trout readily recognizes as the behavior of many hatching insects.

You may see a swirl or a flash of color near your fly at any time, but most often the fish will rush as the fly approaches the surface. If there is no strike, you let the fly float along a few feet more, imitating another characteristic of many insects.

When the trout strikes, set the hook—but *not* with a sharp jerk. A lift of the wrist will do it—at the instant you see the flash of color or swirl near the surface. If the fish you hook at the rock is big, it will be several minutes before you can attempt netting him safely. Since he is familiar with all the aspects of the pool, you can expect him to surge toward the logs, a haven where he has gained freedom often, probably, when less circumspect anglers hooked him from the wrong bank. If he heads for the logs, exert pressure on the rod and try to steer him away. Should he get under them, he may sulk there only briefly and, hopefully, come out the way he went in. Your pressure should be firm but not excessive. Success with a big trout often depends on such small matters.

But even if he does not get into the driftwood, the trout with his full strength can cause you trouble at any time by surfacing and rolling. During a surface roll, you relax rod pressure to avoid breaking the leader or tearing the hook out. If he turns toward the driftwood area of deep, fast water, encourage him to leave the pool by steering him firmly into the avenue of fast water leading downstream. Follow him down, rod held high to keep as much line as possible out of the water as he strips it and part of the backing from the reel. You still have to play him out, recover lost line and bring him to net, but at this point, with nothing save open, easy-moving water between you and the fish, the strategic battle is won.

In this situation, you have avoided the old bugaboo,

drag, presented your fly more temptingly to the trout and minimized the hazards of the stream. The big trout of the pool is your reward for planning the whole campaign well.

TACTICS FOR QUIET WATER

As free of obstacles as a swimming pool, the long, deep flat in the drawing on pages 40–41 presents few problems once a trout is hooked, but it is a good test of your tactical skills. Bright sunlight in this clear water exposes trout to their enemies so well that, unless a stiff breeze ruffles the surface, desirable fish are seldom active during the day. Early in the morning or in late afternoon, when dim light prevails, such water will yield trout. Small fish may venture up from the bottom or out from the banks for a fly at any time of day, but the larger trout seek cover under the bushes along the left bank or hide in the shadows or beneath the grass-covered, undercut bank on the right.

You may often hook trout in such water regardless of breeze or time of day with a technique used by the ancient Greeks and later by English anglers, who called it "dapping with a Flye." In dapping on this stream, your target is the trout concealed near the bank. On a bank where the trout is virtually underfoot, naturally you must step lightly to avoid vibrations. You stand as far back as possible to keep your shadow from the water. Then, using a fly that imitates such favorite trout food as the black ant, with a short line or only the leader hanging from the rod tip, you touch your fly gently to the grass at the bank edge and allow it to fall naturally from the grass to the water. Dapping is delicate, oftentimes blind fishing: the slightest movement of the leader is significant. Large trout often sip in the fly silently and splash only after they feel the hook.

Playing a fish here, where there are no logs, rocks or fast water, is largely a matter of keeping the fish away from

roots and out of the pockets under the bank. After a fish is hooked, you improve your chances of netting the fish by stepping into the shallows near the bank. Although advanced, more sophisticated anglers may look down on dapping as "cheating," the fisherman who enjoys hooking, playing and netting trout will not ignore this method as a way of taking his fish.

When no insects are visible but you see fish rising under the bushes along the left bank, it is quite possible that they are feeding on tiny midges. Tie on a small Black Gnat

and use a tippet no larger than 4x. With a side-arm cast, put your fly in under the bushes upstream from the spot where you have seen a fish rise. As your fly nears the fish, be ready to lift your rod tip on the slightest provocation. Your fly will be on or just beneath the surface and any slight sign near your fly should be interpreted as a striking fish.

On an overcast day good-sized fish may feed on flies hatching or drifting at various depths anywhere in this stretch of stream. Fishing a sunken fly representing the insects you see in the air is a reasonable tactic at such

CURRENT ⟹

times. A long, fine leader and a light line are important: finesse and delicacy in presenting your fly are a vital part of your strategy. On smooth, clear water a slight ripple is very noticeable, and a heavy line or leader will cast stark shadows on the bottom.

TRICKS IN MIXED WATER

In water like that shown in the above drawing, you may fish a wet fly first at the surface, a tactic that might bring

a trout in a splashing surface rise such as dry-fly fishermen cherish. The fast main current sweeps past the outer side of the half-submerged boulder in the stream. Inshore from this boulder is inviting, productive water—a collecting area for insects flying against, or blown against, the rock bluff edging the stream. Logically, fish often lie in this relatively quiet backwater, waiting for such easy pickings.

Though most anglers believe wet flies should be tied on heavy hooks, many patterns may be tied on light wire hooks so that they drop lightly to the surface, float for a few moments and respond more realistically to the changing forces of the water. May flies, sedge flies, stone flies and ants touch the water lightly and often float momentarily, until pulled down in a swirl of water. They move wherever the current may take them—into an eddy or a backwater, down behind a boulder and up again. Many insects, caught temporarily in the current, are submerged only to rise to the surface again, float along low in the water and crawl back to safety on a limb or rock.

In fishing a collecting area where insects drop, it is a smart trick to use a fly tied on a light wire hook, and barely touch it to the water on your first cast or two. On the piece of water in that drawing, you would try the very edge of the stream, along the base of the bluff. Touch the fly briefly and withdraw it. In this way you may tease and excite trout. Then, after false-casting once or twice to dry the fly, permit it to float on the surface film for a few feet downstream over any eager trout that might be lying there.

The current on both sides of the half-submerged boulder (see page 42 again) is strong, and any trout there is probably holding close to the boulder. Here you can make the rock itself work for you. A fly cast upstream sweeps by too fast to have much effect. Since there may be trout feeding out in the fast water, one approach is to cast your fly upstream, and as it drifts down guide it toward the area below the boulder. Here, where there is less direct pull of the current, the churning water of the eddy will activate the hackles of a sunken fly. Another approach is to cast your fly into the pocket of water below the boulder so that your leader falls across the rock. In this position the fly may float and move free of drag. This tactic is often useful with dry as well as wet flies.

In fast water so characteristic of a western stream a heavy wire hook is often good for sinking the fly to greater depths, where trout often feed. Bear this in mind the next time you visit a tackle store. For if you equip yourself with hooks of varying weights you will have both a light touch on the surface and also an effective lure in the depths.

FISHING A BIG POOL

A trout stream may brawl through canyons and run fast and wide in shallows; but here or there, sooner or later, almost all streams slow down and for a moment lose their force in a large, deep pool. In these pools the normal food lanes all but disappear. The water is calm and looks easy to fish; but such pools hold challenges, testing the angler's casting skill and his knowledge both of fish behavior and of insect behavior above and below the surface.

Desirable trout often rest during the day in the deepest water, difficult to reach with the small flies which some anglers prefer for this type of fishing. In such water the angler must fish far and fine, not only lengthening his casts to reach the more distant points but also using extra-long leaders, tapered to 4x, 5x or even 6x and tied to nymph-like flies of the smallest sizes. To the casual fisherman these minute particles of feather and fur may appear laughable, but as an angler matures on the streams he comes to appreciate their value in winning trout.

At dawn and dusk, trout stream insects often become quite active. Hatching flymphs swim upward through the water, take wing, fly about to mate, then drop to the surface, where the females deposit their eggs. During a hatch at dusk, particularly, the surface of a pool is broken by the swirls of feeding fish. The novice assumes the trout are feeding on floating flies. Quite often he is right; this can be the dry-fly fisherman's finest hour. Equally as often, however, the angler may be mystified and frustrated; he sees trout swirling everywhere, yet his dry fly floats along untouched. Why? In this whirl of activity, when trout seem to be feeding on floating insects, they are often feasting on swimming flymphs just beneath the surface, an inch or so below the domain of the dry-fly fisherman. There in the dim light of dusk the trout are safe from

45

Fishing a Big Pool

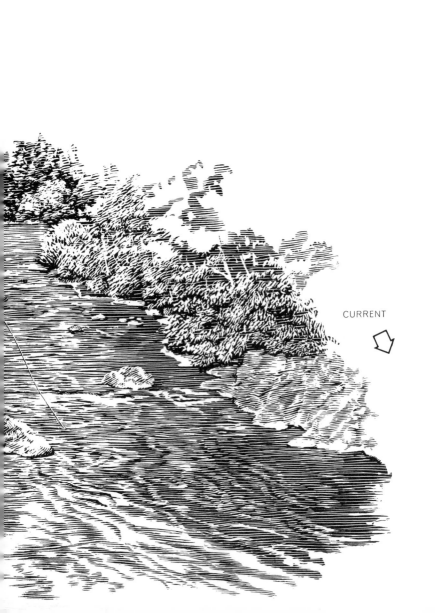

CURRENT

all their enemies except the angler skilled in the use of the lifelike flymph.

Such an angler was Jim Leisenring, whose deadliest technique is the one he evolved to use with a flymph close to the surface. Here, in fact virtually at the surface, at the crucial moment of the insect's metamorphosis into the mature fly, the essential drama between insect and trout takes place with greatest intensity. The heart of this drama is the sudden exposure to the trout's view of a hatching insect struggling upward naturally and about to escape.

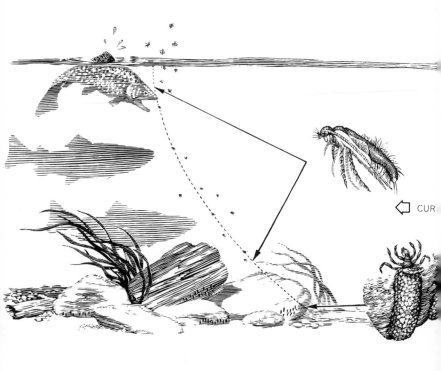

CUR

Many species of insects emerge from cases or from hiding places among stones and swim upward through the current in a curving path toward the surface. Trout feed on ascending pupae or other insect nymphs in the depths far more often than casual anglers realize: the angler notices it only when a trout swirls and splashes to take an insect close to the surface.

Leisenring, in fact, learned early in his career that this phenomenon of escaping, free-swimming insects, like the caddis pupa shown enlarged in the drawing opposite, was so exciting to trout that an imitation of the action could be used not only during a hatch in a pool, but almost any time of day, wherever an angler can maneuver a sunken fly naturally. This favorite technique of his—called the "Leisenring Lift"—is executed by maneuvering line and fly in the water as shown in the drawing on pages 50–51.

The Leisenring Lift, used wherever the speed of the current is not excessive, imitates the behavior of a hatching flymph. To execute the lift, cast upstream and allow the fly to sink. Then, as the fly nears the position of the trout, raise arm and rod gradually to cause the fly to lift naturally through the currents. The trout may take it at once or he may hesitate and inspect the fly as he follows it downstream momentarily, making his decisive move just before the fly escapes at the surface. Stream strategy, finesse and a delicate control of the fly are the decisive factors in the Leisenring Lift.

Leisenring Lift

4
Learning to Cast

AS in most forms of angling, the first essential of fly fishing is competent casting. Though obvious to anyone who has done any sort of fresh-water casting, it is worth stating here that accuracy rather than distance is the initial goal. Distance will come in time. Meanwhile the novice who masters accurate casts of 35 feet will take fish on almost any stream.

When you first attempt the basic overhead cast (pages 58–62), you will go through the motions in a simple, mechanical way. Gradually your casts will become a graceful, rhythmic, fluid action executed subconsciously, much as a sports car driver shifts gears by "feel," unmindful of the mechanics involved. To carry the analogy a step further, your choice of fly rod is as purposeful a decision as is a driver's choice of car: your rod commits you to a certain action and style.

A fly rod with stiff action is usually the choice of the dry-fly man, who prefers heavy line enabling him to cast greater distances. A softer-action rod, due to the smoothness and evenness of the action and the sensitivity inherent in it, is traditionally preferred by anglers fishing the delicate wet fly. If your aim is to become versatile with one rod that will be suitable for a variety of conditions, you will select one of medium action. With such a sensitive yet powerful all-purpose rod, you can cast a dry or a wet fly by merely changing the fly and the leader connecting it to the line. Medium-action rods from 7 to 9 feet long are available in either bamboo or glass.

But the fishing site must also be considered. For small streams, where distance is secondary to accuracy, the shorter, lighter rod is preferable, affording you a maximum of sport. On large streams and lakes, where distance is often necessary, the longer rod is preferable because of its greater power.

In the choice between manually operated and automatic reels, the simpler, manual, narrow-frame reel is perhaps preferable. The automatic reel retrieves line at the touch of a finger, and some anglers want this time-saving feature when fishing big water. Whichever you choose, your reel should not be so heavy that you notice its weight while casting, yet large enough to hold casting line and 50 yards of backing line for playing large fish.

Although there is a detailed analysis of lines and leaders in Chapter 5 (pages 71–74), a brief discussion is nevertheless in order here. When you first try the overhead cast on a lawn, you should select a line that works well with your rod. Of the various types of lines used in fly fishing, double-tapered line is unquestionably the best for all-round effectiveness. Double-tapered line starts with a small diameter at one end, gradually increases thickness to a mid-section of larger diameter, then tapers off again at the other end. Only one tapered end and the level mid-section serve in a cast—when the casting end becomes worn, reverse the line and use the other end.

Double-tapered lines come in a variety of thicknesses and, in general, the thicker, heavier lines are easier to cast.

But here, since the only critic that counts is the trout, a compromise is necessary. From the trout's point of view, a fine, light line is better. It touches and enters the water with a minimum of disturbance, is itself less noticeable in the water and casts less shadow on the bottom. All such disturbances may register on the trout's radar. The popular line calipering .045 inch in the mid-section and tapered to .025 inch at the ends is easy to cast, but some anglers prefer a lighter line tapering from .035 inch to .020 inch. The synthetic leaders today, of nylon or platyl, are tapered, the smallest diameter being the end section, or tippet, to which the fly is attached. Again, deferring to the sensitivity of the trout, many skillful anglers recommend a light leader, 8 or 9 feet long, tapering from .013 to .006 inch at the farthermost end—the tippet.

Just because some master anglers lay down exacting requirements for equipment, you need not infer that either you or the equipment must be just perfect before you will take fish. It is reassuring to know that experts stress the importance of short, accurate casts—such as you will first learn—as the best way, by and large, to take fish. The angler should make as short a cast as the situation permits, not only to maintain accuracy but to enable the fly to touch the water before the leader and to minimize slack in the line. Some experts have maintained that the moment when a fly touches is the only moment at which a trout will take an artificial fly for a live one. There are other important moments. Later on we will cover the techniques evolved to create such moments. For the present, your first step is to take rod in hand and practice the cast.

THE GRIP

To achieve a proper grip for casting, hold your hand palm up and lay the rod handle across the second joints of the fingers. Close your hand and rotate the wrist until

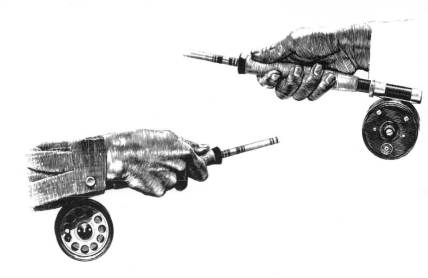

the hand is in the position shown in the two drawings above. Press your thumb down on the handle. Be sure to keep the thumb on top; its placement is essential in melding your action to that of the rod. Notice that the rod is gripped so that the reel extends below the hand in a vertical plane.

The position of the opposite hand (that is, the left

hand of a right-handed caster) is also important; the angler constantly uses it to increase or decrease the amount of line in the air, on the water or in the water. This hand is also used to retrieve line when maneuvering a wet fly. As you start the overhead cast, the line should be hanging in a slack loop, held by the opposite hand at waist level, as shown in the drawing at the bottom of page 56.

THE OVERHEAD CAST

The overhead cast is the first one you learn because it is the method of presenting a fly that you will use most often. Moreover, it embodies the same basic principles as the side-arm cast and the forward part of the roll cast, which you will learn later. Many experts used to cast with the elbow pressed against the side, most of the power stemming from the wrist. The modern technique advocated here, however, involving freer action of the whole arm, gives greater accuracy and is less tiring to the wrist.

The arm, wrist and hand move much as they would if you were hammering a nail, with wrist movement minimized to maintain control of the rod and preserve accuracy. When actually presenting a fly to the water, you execute the complete action shown in the following sequence. To feed out more line or to dry a fly you will often "false-cast." This involves following the action through the fourth illustration, on page 61, but beginning a second backcast just before the fly touches the water. If you are lengthening line, in the forward part of each false cast you release some or all of the line you have been holding in your opposite hand.

To start, strip out 15 to 20 feet of line through the rod guides and lay it out straight on a lawn. Then, gripping the rod and holding a slack loop of line with your opposite hand, as you have learned, you face in the direction of the line running across the lawn. At the start of the cast you

should be holding the fly rod in such a way that the tip is raised slightly above a line parallel to the ground.

Slowly raise the rod by lifting the upper arm and at the same time bending the elbow to bring the forearm toward your face. At this point the opposite hand holds the line securely so that no slack line slips through the guides as you raise the rod. With the illustration on page 59 and with each subsequent illustration in this action sequence are diagrams of the lively, whiplike action of the rod and

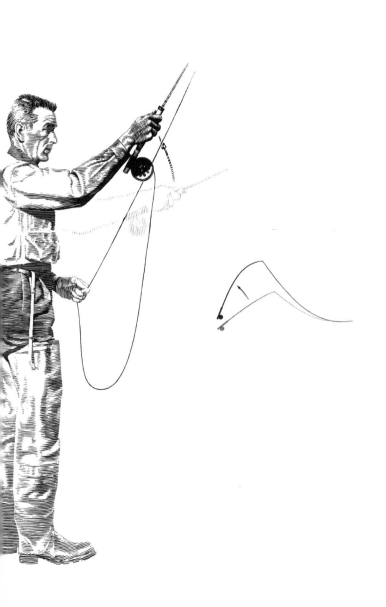

the flowing course your line will follow through the air when you learn to execute the actions reasonably well.

The third step in the overhead cast is to lift the line up off the ground. As you slowly raise the rod, when your forearm and rod are at an angle of about 45° to the ground (*shadow outline*), give a smart lift and then immediately stop when the forearm is nearly vertical. If you do this smoothly, the line will rise from the ground and

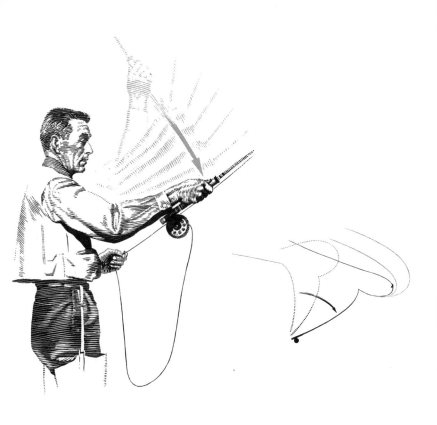

move up and back. As the line continues backward, re-lax the wrist somewhat so that the rod drifts backward slightly. You will feel a tug as the line straightens out behind you.

The forward part of the cast begins as soon as the line straightens out behind. The instant this happens, slowly start to lower the upper arm while pushing forward with the forearm. Through the flection of the rod you will feel that you are pulling the line forward. As the movement continues, the rod enters the power zone. When your arm and rod approach the 45° position, push hard with your thumb and wrist. This causes the upper part of the rod to drive the line forward in a very tight loop.

As the line straightens out in front of you, release the slack line held by your other hand and the momentum pulls it forward through the guides. As the line shoots through the guides, your rod should be back at starting position. As the line falls, raise the rod tip slightly. This will not only put the fly down better, but the slight angle gives you a margin of safety: the flection of the rod cushions the shock if a trout hits immediately. A fish with a direct pull on the line very likely will break the tippet.

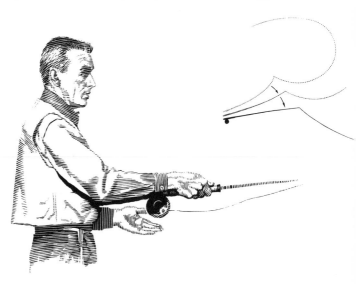

THE SIDE-ARM CAST

Often trees or high banks or other obstructions along a stream prevent you from executing the back part of an overhead cast. In such cases, where there is clearance to the side, you can cast side-arm so that the line travels over the water in a horizontal plane rather than vertically overhead. In side-arm casts you forfeit some accuracy and dis-

tance, but you can usually maneuver into a position that will allow you to present the fly in likely spots to take fish. In some cases, even when there is overhead clearance behind you, the side-arm is the only way of getting a fly under brushy overhang and other inaccessible places favored by trout and too often ignored by casual anglers. In steep canyons, too, when the wind is running strong, side-arm casts can help you by keeping the line low over the water.

The grip for the side-arm cast is similar to that for overhead casting, except that your rod and hand are rotated

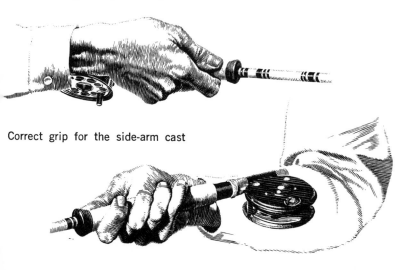

Correct grip for the side-arm cast

Close-up of the side-arm cast

about 90°. Thus, the thumb is no longer on top but to the outside, lying in the plane of the horizontal sweeping action you are about to perform. As the hand is rotated to effect this position, the reel now lies nearly horizontal. Discounting the slight effect gravity has on a line moving horizontally, the course of your line in the horizontal plane when you cast side-arm is identical to the course of the line in the vertical plane when you cast overhead. You can begin learning the side-arm cast on a lawn or on a stream. If you start on a stream you should first try it in an open area, where you can pay out some line first with overhead casts. Then, when you have the side-arm cast learned at least mechanically, you can try it in an obstructed area, where a good deal more finesse will be required.

At the start, you face the direction in which you intend to cast, with the casting arm extended but not straight or stiff. Your upper arm should be sloping down at an angle of about 45°, the forearm and rod extended and slanting up a few degrees from horizontal. If you are a right-hander your rod and forearm should be pointing a little to the right of the direction in which you intend to cast.

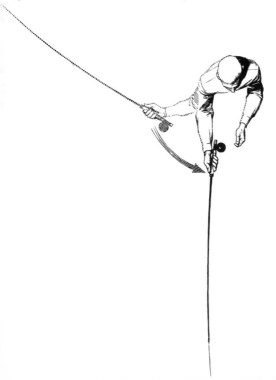

In the side-arm cast, as shown in the drawing looking down on the caster, page 65, swing your arm back until your forearm and rod reach a point roughly at right angles to the starting position. As you start this backward sweep, your wrist should be stiff so that forearm and rod move as a unit. But about midway in the sweep back, you flex your wrist to the rear to power the line backward. When the line straightens out behind you—you will feel the tug on the rod—begin the forward cast, sweeping arm and rod back toward the starting position. In the first part of the return arc, the wrist remains flexed rearward. About midway, by straightening the wrist and pressing with your thumb, you shove the rod forward. This action, as in the overhead cast, will cause the rod tip to flip the line in a tight loop toward the intended target.

THE ROLL CAST

The roll cast is a particular necessity when trees or other obstructions do not give you clearance for either overhead or side-arm casts. It can also be useful in placing a fly at a point directly upwind from the fisherman. Beyond these obvious values, there are others: there is a minimum of arm and rod movement to telegraph your presence to the fish, and in fishing a submerged fly the film of water on fly and leader is less disturbed by the roll cast, so that both sink more cleanly as they are put down on the surface. Also, when fishing deep, often you tempt fish by causing your fly to rise. You do this by raising your rod vertically, and from this position the most convenient cast is another roll cast. For other reasons equally important, which were covered in the discussion of stream strategy (see Chapter 3), the roll cast, although not so accurate as other casts, nor as good for distance, is a valuable part of your casting repertoire.

In the roll cast, as the name implies and the next sequence indicates, you draw the line toward you as you raise your rod. Then with a sudden motion of the arm you roll the line back out over the water. While you can start learning the overhead and side-arm casts on a lawn, you should start trying the roll cast on a stream or, better yet, on a still pond, where the smooth, even resistance of the water against the line helps achieve a satisfactory cast.

For the roll cast you take the same grip on the rod as for the overhead cast. Start with about 20 feet of line on the water at your feet, preferably on the side of your casting arm. Keep 3 or 4 feet of line slack between your other hand and the reel, as shown in the drawing below. From this simple beginning you can make casts of up to 50 feet, following the sequence of action explained here, using the other hand to strip out more line from the reel at the completion of each cast.

As you begin the roll cast, the wrist is held stiff, as in the overhead, so that forearm and rod are a single working unit. At the start of a cast, lift the rod by raising your upper arm and forearm as shown in the drawing below. You carry this motion on through at a *slow* speed until the forearm and rod are overhead and actually inclining slightly to the rear. At this point you should make a definite pause so that the line, which has been pulled toward you through the water, now hangs slack near your side. The wrist should remain slightly relaxed.

Forward movement of the cast is started by lowering the upper arm suddenly while pushing forward with the forearm. Give a thrust with the thumb as the arm moves forward, as in the overhead cast, so that the rod tip will flip the line into a curling loop which will roll out over the water. The rod and line action for the start of the forward cast are shown in shadow. Final movements of rod and line are above.

5
Lines, Leaders and Knots

IF you care to, you can begin learning the side-arm cast on a stream or pond rather than a lawn. In any case, the third cast in your repertoire, the roll cast shown on pages 66–69, can best be learned on a stream. There you will need to know how to tie the knots joining line, leader and fly. So here, before you reach the water, are some facts to guide you.

LINES

Of the types of line available, we recommend double-taper floating line as the best for general use. Single-taper line offers the same casting characteristics but has a shorter life since the angler cannot reverse it when one end begins to wear. Level line, as the name implies, has no taper.

71

Though cheaper, it is not recommended. The most that can be said for level line is that it will do in various situations, but is not really good in any. Another type, weight-forward or torpedo-head line, has a thick, heavy section near the forward end which pulls the rest of the line through the guides more readily. Designed for distance, weight-forward line will cast accurately but with less finesse than the more delicate double-taper. The makeup of the various types of lines generally used in fly fishing is as shown in the diagram below.

LINES

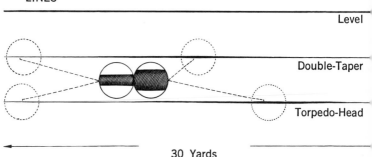

Level

Double-Taper

Torpedo-Head

30 Yards

Unless your line is carefully matched to the particular characteristics of your fly rod, you will never be able to cast with full effectiveness. There are few decisions more important, with regard to equipment, than the purchase of line of the correct weight for your rod. Many rod manufacturers specify the appropriate line for each of their rods, but if you are not sure what weight to choose, consult a knowledgeable person in a tackle shop, bringing your rod with you. The AFTMA (American Fishing Tackle Manufacturers Association) standard designations are shown in the table below. Floating line is preferred as the general-purpose fly line and may be used for wet flies and nymphs on most streams and lakes. Sinking line is for special conditions when you need to

72

fish a fly very deep. The dry fly is, of course, fished exclusively with the floating line. Many anglers have—certainly for any extending fishing trip—two or three sets of balanced rod and line combinations for various types of water.

AFTMA Flyline Standards, Symbols and Types

Designation Number	STANDARDS Weight in Grains * (437 ½ gr. =103)	Range (Manufacturers' tolerances)	FLYLINE SYMBOLS	FLYLINE TYPES
1	60	54– 66	L=Level	F=Floating
2	80	74– 86	DT=Double-	S=Sinking
3	100	94–106	taper	I=Intermediate
4	120	114–126	WF=Weight-	(Float or Sink)
5	140	134–146	forward	
6	160	152–168	ST=Single	
7	185	177–193	taper	
8	210	202–218		
9	240	230–250		
10	280	270–290		
11	330	318–342		
12	380	368–392		

* Weight is based upon the first 30 feet of line exclusive of taper or tip. Example: DT-5-F is a double-taper line No. 5 floating line weighing 140 grains.

LEADERS

An understanding of the characteristics of leaders is important in all fly fishing. The principal types of leader material used today are synthetics such as nylon, platyl and perlyl. Whatever the material, it is important that the leader does not glisten or glare in sunlight.

The flotation of synthetic leaders can be reduced by rubbing them with soap, mud, or the slime from a fish. To offset lightness some anglers tie up synthetic leaders with a torpedo head or "belly" of larger diameter toward the center sections of the leader, offsetting the overall lightness of the leader by adding some weight at the point where it serves best to help carry the fly forward.

To ensure against slipping, knots in the synthetics must be tied with extra care. Low temperatures may cause these materials to become brittle, and crack or break.

In general, heavier leaders serve well when fishing rough water, when using a large fly and when casting into or across a strong wind. Lighter leaders are essential in still, clear water, and when casting a small fly, and under bright, sunny conditions when even the slight shadow cast by the semi-translucent leader can be enough to spook the wary trout.

As with line, more delicacy of presentation is achieved with a tapered rather than with a level leader. The thicker end of a tapered leader is connected to the line; the smaller end, the tippet, is tied to the fly. Today, knotless, tapered synthetic leaders are the most popular, although some anglers prefer knotted leaders made up of 10- or 12-inch lengths of different thicknesses, tied in diminishing sequence to achieve a taper. Leader material varies in thickness and also in strength. Thicknesses are designated as 2x, 3x, 4x and so forth, with "x" equaling .010 inch, 1x equaling .009 inch, 2x equaling .008 inch, and so on.

LEADERS

Level

Tapered

Knotted-Tapered

9 Feet

KNOTS

Of the variety of knots that anglers use, those illustrated below will do the whole job of combining all of the essential elements as you normally will use them.

Perfection loop. With this loop tied in the end of the leader, you will need only a simple jam knot to connect leader to line. Loop should be about ½ inch in diameter.

Jam knot. Here is a simple, fast and reliable way of connecting the line to the perfection loop tied in the end of the leader.

Blood knot. Used to join sections of level leader material of varying thicknesses in diminishing order for a tapered leader.

Turle knot. Used to connect the leader tippet to the fly. In using gut, the knot is tied as it is shown here; but with platyl or nylon, in order to prevent any slipping, tuck the end back through loop once more before drawing the knot tight, thus making a double-turle knot.

HOOKS

The quality of the hook is vital since the fly is only as good as the hook upon which it is tied. Soft hooks bend, brittle hooks break, so the temper of a hook is a prime consideration. You should test each box of hooks by bending one hook in a vise. To penetrate a trout's jaw, the point should be sharp; the barb, small. Hook styles and shapes are a matter of preference. Model Perfect and Sproat are most popular today. On the next page, hook sizes 10 to 20 shown for the Model Perfect style are the sizes you will use most in imitating stream insects.

HOOK STYLES AND SHAPES

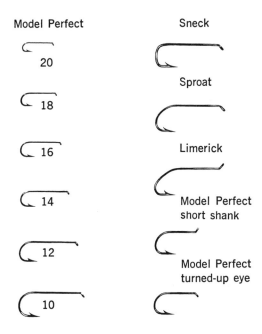

Model Perfect

20

18

16

14

12

10

Sneck

Sproat

Limerick

Model Perfect
short shank

Model Perfect
turned-up eye

6
Nymph Fishing

BY definition all nymphs are larva of aquatic insects and resemble, to some extent, the winged insects they will become after they mature. As nymphs they have no wings, of course, and burrow into the silt or vegetation and hide in the gravel or natural debris on or near the stream bed. According to their habitat and method of locomotion, nymphs have been divided into four categories: burrowers, swimmers, clamberers and crawlers.

Trout feed on these nymphs at all stages of their development, methodically searching the stream bed for nymphs or nymph cases on stones or aquatic plants. Artificial nymphs fished deep are often effective, therefore, early in the season when the water is high or discolored from the spring runoffs. They are also effective later in the season when there is no insect activity on the surface of a stream or lake.

Nymphs should be fished to sink and move naturally with the currents. Cast upstream or diagonally up and across the stream. A fish may take the nymph at any time during

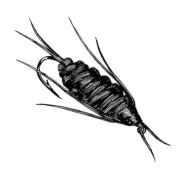

Dark Mossback Nymph

the drift, but most fish are hooked as the nymph reaches the lower end of a drift and just prior to your retrieve. The swing with the current causes the nymph to rise in a manner that attracts the fish.

Nymph fishing in lakes often requires a fast-sinking or extra-fast-sinking line to get the lure down into the feeding zone of the fish. A rather slow retrieve with frequent pauses will cause the nymph to ascend and descend in a lifelike manner. At times the angler must experiment with various speeds of retrieves and at various depths in order to succeed. Once you discover a combination acceptable to the trout, you will do well, as a rule, if you repeat the presentation exactly as before. Such minor considerations are often decisive in nymph fishing.

Although nymph patterns have not been standardized as much as dry flies and wet flies, some of the more popular patterns today include the following: Little Yellow Stone Nymph, Green Damsel Nymph, Gray Damsel Nymph, March Brown Nymph, Black Drake Nymph, Montana Nymph, Dark Mossback Nymph and the Olive May-fly Nymph.

Olive May-fly Nymph

7
The Dry Fly

FISHING a floating fly is an extremely popular technique because the angler can always see the fly and the rise of a fish as he wades upstream exploring the water with casts aimed somewhat above the water so the delicate fly may drop naturally and easily to the surface. Accuracy and finesse in presenting a dry fly to a large fish feeding at intervals on floating insects will test the nerve and skill of a novice. This is referred to as "fishing the rise," in contrast to "fishing the water" during those lulls or periods of inactivity when no fish are seen feeding at the surface.

Before the dry fly is allowed to drop to the water the angler makes several false casts to dry the fly. False casts also pose and answer two vital questions: Is there ample clearance of weeds, brush or trees for your backcast? and— equally important—Is the amount of line coiled in your left hand and moving in the air adequate for reaching the exact piece of water you have chosen to place your fly? With or without a wind blowing against or across or with the direction of your cast, false casts are essential preliminary tactics for the angler fishing upstream, downstream or across the stream.

Just as sudden changes in the direction or velocity of the wind may force the dry-fly angler to pause or stop fishing momentarily, the appearance of a large trout feeding in another section of a pool or a riffle may suggest a minor or major change in stream strategy. Catch the smaller trout feeding recklessly if you must. Move promptly, however, into position for deceiving the larger fish which will be more selective and more challenging. This may involve cutting back your leader from the 1-pound to the 2-pound section—a length of 8 or 10 inches, as a rule. It may involve changing to a fresh new fly, and it can often indicate a change in your position in the river for the most advantageous presentation of your fly to this desirable fish.

A methodical, deliberate approach to fishing the dry fly can be productive, of course, but versatility and awareness of changing or new opportunities are always the hallmarks of an imaginative, experienced fly fisherman. The changes involve, for example, the appearance of one or more insects during the course of an afternoon or evening; sudden variations in the weather; constant new problems encountered in moving along pools, around rocks or log jams or bridges; and incidental information you pick up from other fishermen or by examining the stomachs of trout. These and other factors can have a direct bearing on the many decisions and choices open to a dry-fly fisherman moving up or down a stream.

USING THE WIND

The dry fly activated by the wind is often irresistible to trout. Even in ordinarily tranquil pools the surface is broken enough to lower the chances of a fish seeing you or your leader. You are able, therefore, to move in and fish with a shorter line, often from the bank near a hot spot. With a short length of line and the leader extending from the rod, let the wind skitter and bounce the dry fly on and off the water. In certain circumstances a longer line can be used with the rod held high and moved to shift your fly from one feeding lane to another or along the edges of floating or sunken logs.

CASTING UPSTREAM

Ideally, present your fly above and to the side of a feeding fish so that it does not see either your leader or your line. Always let your fly float several feet downstream from the fish before lifting the fly from the water. The fish may be following it, as they often do in fast water, and be about to take it. Also, there may be another fish below ready to take a jaunty floating insect moving naturally with the current. The rule, then, is to fish out every cast until the fly begins to drag or move unnaturally.

The retrieve of your dry fly should be made slowly to avoid disturbing the water or wetting the fly unnecessarily.

Retrieving Line

Assuming you are standing in the water and have cast upstream at a slight angle, reach up and take the line between your thumb and forefinger just below the first line guide on your fly rod. Depending on the speed of the fly floating toward you, pull the line through the guides to remove or avoid any slack line between the end of your rod and the fly. As the line is pulled in, catch it beneath the forefinger of your hand holding the fly rod. This ensures a minimum of slack line between your rod tip and any fish rising to your fly. Although a certain number of fish may virtually hook themselves, far more will eject the fly unless the angler reacts instantly by raising the rod tip to set the hook. For this reason slack line must be avoided and controlled.

Some anglers prefer to coil the retrieved line in loops in their left hand while others let the line float downstream behind them. Steelhead fishermen place the retrieved line in a stripping basket on their belt. Careful handling of retrieved line, in any event, has other advantages that cannot be ignored by any angler: you are always prepared for perfect shooting of the line on your next cast, and your line will flow smoothly through the guides during the first powerful run of any big fish.

CASTING DOWNSTREAM

In various situations, especially above natural obstacles, a dry fly must be floated downstream from the angler to the fish. Here, an important advantage for the angler is that the fish will see the fly before it sees the leader since it is facing upstream. However, rather than retrieve line, the angler must carefully release it to avoid excessive slack line at the instant of a strike.

One tactic useful in open water is a rather high cast above a feeding fish and a sharp pull on the rod which brings the fly back upstream and allows the line to fall to the water in a series of s-shaped loops. Depending on the current or cross-currents, you may mend your line or release more line as required to float the fly into the feeding zone of the fish.

The downstream float beneath overhanging brush or branches is often very effective because such places offer fine protection for trout as well as a constant supply of food. Both aquatic and terrestrial insect imitations can be used since grasshoppers, beetles and ants frequently fall to the water here and fish often rise to sip these into their mouths, causing only a small dimple on the water. Unless the angler is alert for this almost imperceptible rise, he will miss the fish. Or, should the fish hook itself, the prize can be easily and instantly lost in the brush or the roots beneath the water. In setting the hook in such fish the angler should keep his rod tip near the water to avoid jerking the fly up into the branches when the fish misses the fly or strikes short.

One of the most exciting and dramatic moments in fly fishing is the initial float of a dry fly to a large trout feeding at the upper edge of a log jam. Like many large fish, they often rise at rather predictable intervals ranging from 10 to 20 seconds when flies are plentiful during a hatch. This suggests, as a rule, that your fly should arrive some few seconds after the fish has taken a fly. Also, if the fish is over 3 or 4 pounds, you must be prepared to exert strong pressure immediately to keep the fish from the logs. Once the fish is out in the open currents, hold your rod high and let him run against the line on your reel, retrieving line at intervals between runs without undue pressure at any time unless he goes toward the log jam.

Retrieving Line

At the end of a downstream float of the dry fly, the retrieve of your fly must be made slowly to avoid disturbing the water. Before retrieving or during the retrieve a hesitant fish may be tempted to strike by twitching the fly, especially in rather rough or broken water. In any event, steer the fly away from the more promising water during the retrieve. With a floating line you can lift line, leader and fly with a sharp backcast after retrieving all but 20 or 25 feet of line. Make several false casts to dry the fly and you are ready for another presentation.

8

Choice of Flies

ALL dry flies represent winged insects and most dry flies represent either the May fly or the caddis fly. Also, most dry-fly patterns are direct imitations of natural insects— *deceivers* rather than brighter-colored *attractors*. Both types of flies catch fish, but the more orthodox, conventional *deceivers* deserve the attention of the beginner far more than the *attractors*, which seem to appeal to fishermen more than to the fish, especially browns and rainbows.

The bright-colored Parmachene Belle (scarlet, white and yellow) is effective when fishing for brook trout and landlocked salmon in Maine and eastern Canada, but the more natural colorings of blue-gray, brown, ginger or cream are far more appealing to brown trout, rainbow trout and cutthroat trout. Steelhead and salmon, however, definitely prefer brighter and more colorful *attractor* flies.

Other important distinctions to be made in selecting dry flies are to be made according to the rivers or lakes you will fish and, to some extent, your personal preferences for delicate, lifelike flies, durability, buoyancy or visibility. No single pattern possesses all four qualities, any one or two of which can be decisive in catching fish under certain conditions.

TYPES OF DRY FLIES

Divided Wing Flies suggest the May fly floating along shortly after its emergence from the water. Imitations should have stiff hackles, delicate tapered bodies, stiff tail fibers and natural proportions with balance in order to float properly. Some popular patterns are Quill Gordon, Blue Dun, Adams, March Brown, Light Cahill and Ginger Quill.

Blue Dun

Downwing Flies suggest caddis flies, stone flies and grasshoppers that have dropped to the water. Stiff hackles and wings that slope back above the rather prominent body are the important features of this fly. Some popular patterns are Gray Sedge, King's River Caddis, Bucktail Caddis, Orange or Yellow Stone-Fly and the Hopper Fly.

Joe's Hopper

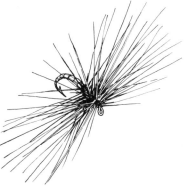

Skater Spider

Spider and Variant Flies suggest any insect, especially delicate insects, because they are tied on rather small hooks with relatively long, stiff hackles which drop so lightly on the surface that a slight breeze can cause them to twitch or jump. Some popular patterns are Badger Variant, Ginger Spider, Multicolor Variant and Blue Dun Spider.

Hairwing Flies suggest many types of insects and provide the three important advantages of buoyancy, durability and, in most patterns, good visibility. Some popular patterns are Hairwing Coachman, Hairwing Royal Coachman, Gray Wulff, Grizzly Wulff and Blonde Wulff.

Bi-Visible Flies also suggest many types of insects and offer both buoyancy and visibility. Most effective in fast, rough or broken water with natural float, bouncing or skittering near the edges of the current. Always tied with one white hackle at the front of the hook for visibility. Some popular patterns are Brown, Blue Dun, Badger and Grizzly.

Brown Bi-Visible

Hairbodied Flies are tied with bodies of clipped deer hair to represent any of the larger insects. Extremely buoyant in the roughest water, the bodies are very durable and the wings are usually quite visible. Some popular patterns are the Irresistible, Humpy and Rat-Faced McDougall.

Parachute Flies are available in any pattern but the hackles are tied to the base of an upright hairwing and parallel to the shank of the hook. All hackle fibers float, therefore, in or on the surface film in a lifelike manner with good visibility and buoyancy. Some popular patterns are Coachman, Adams, Blue Dun and Light Cahill.

Terrestrial Flies imitate land insects, such as beetles, ants, worms and crickets, that drop to the water. These flies are usually fragile and have poor visibility. Some popular patterns are the Jassid with yellow or orange body, the Inch Worm, Black Ant, Red Ant and Beetle.

Midge Flies represent and suggest very small insects of any kind, some of which have a great appeal to the trout. They have poor visibility, limited durability but rather good buoyancy. Some popular patterns are the Black Gnat, Gray Midge and Cream Midge in sizes 20 and 22, which require 6x or 7x tippets since the eyes of these hooks are very small.

STREAMERS AND BUCKTAILS

When the water is high and discolored many species of fresh-water and salt-water gamefish will take lures that imitate various minnows, fingerlings and baitfish. As a knowledge of insects is useful in fly fishing, some knowledge of the small fish inhabiting the water you plan to fish will be helpful in selecting successful lures. As a rule, streamers and bucktails are cast above likely holding water and retrieved within view of the fish with an erratic, twitching motion that simulates the behavior of an injured minnow.

Such a presentation may appeal to a fish's hunger, rapacity, playfulness or curiosity.

Most streamers and bucktails are bright-colored *attractors* with silver tinsel bodies and color combinations of yellow, orange, red, brown or gray and the shape or form and size of baitfish. *Deceiver* patterns are more carefully designed to imitate specific small fish such as the blacknose dace, smelt, blackstripe minnow, yellow perch or the fingerlings of rainbow, brown or brook trout, salmon and whitefish. Lifelike swimming action is achieved with long feathers in the streamers and long hair in the bucktails, although some patterns combine both feathers and hair in varying amounts. To facilitate hooking a fish, most streamers and bucktails are tied on long-shanked hooks and some are tied tandem on two hooks that are connected by a piece of synthetic leader material.

Regional preferences of fish and fishermen have given great popularity to streamers in New England, especially Maine, and eastern Canada where brook trout and landlocked salmon predominate. Popular patterns include the Gray Ghost Streamer, Mickey Finn Bucktail, Supervisor Streamer and Polar Chub Bucktail. Streamers are used by some anglers in the western states. More popular in the West, however, are the bucktail-winged steelhead flies, which resemble wet flies since they are tied with a hackle and the wing is in a more upright position. Popular patterns in the West include the Spruce Fly Streamer, Polar Chub Bucktail and, in steelhead flies, the Kalama Special, Skykomish Sunrise and Van Luven, Red. Popular salt-water flies fished for coho salmon and cutthroat trout are Howell's Coho and Andy's Coho.